Previously Owned

Also by Nathan McClain

Scale

Previously Owned

Nathan McClain

Four Way Books
Tribeca

For Jessica
and for our children

Library of Congress Cataloging-in-Publication Data

Names: McClain, Nathan, author.
Title: Previously owned / Nathan McClain.
Description: [New York] : Four Way Books, [2022]
Identifiers: LCCN 2022003864 | ISBN 9781954245266 (paperback) | ISBN
9781954245396 (epub)
Subjects: LCGFT: Poetry.
Classification: LCC PS3613.C35724 P74 2022 | DDC 811/.6--dc23
LC record available at https://lccn.loc.gov/2022003864
This book is manufactured in the United States of America and printed on
acid-free paper.

Four Way Books is a not-for-profit literary press. We are grateful for the assistance
we receive from individual donors, public arts agencies, and private foundations
including the NEA, NEA Cares, Literary Arts Emergency Fund, and the
New York State Council on the Arts, a state agency.

PROUD MEMBER

[clmp]

We are a proud member of the Community of Literary Magazines and Presses.

Contents

"If you start your history with slavery, everything since then seems like progress."

—Dr. John Henrik Clarke

"It is difficult
to get the news from poems
                yet men die miserably every day
                        for lack
of what is found there."

—William Carlos Williams, "Asphodel, That Greeny Flower"

"There is a Latin phrase that is indicative of the pastoral: *locus amoenus*, or 'pleasant place.' In the pastoral, we are often urged to associate the country with paradise, but one person's paradise is another person's hell."

—Jennifer Chang

Boy Pulling a Thorn from His Foot

Small enough
to cradle. Caught
in the act of concentration,

you see it, chiseled there,
his bronze body curled into
a question

mark, not pulling,
rather, *about* to pull,
the thorn finally out.

Nothing original here.
Nothing new.
Marble, quartz—the old

masters have, for ages now,
sculpted this scene—you've seen
it—and here you

are, looking.
Again the little boy.
Again his insistent

grief. So what
some exhibits in the museum
have already gone

dark? So what
others have moved on
to new rooms? Left

you comfortless,
with your notepad
and pen. And what

have you learned from
standing here so long
examining pain? No

matter how ancient.
What good
has it done you?

The thorn, thrumming
still. He almost
has it now. So close.

Step back, the guard
warns, his one job
to enforce the distance

necessary, which might be called
perspective, though
not yet.

i.

Mafia Myth

In the town there are townspeople

There is night and there is day

This is never not the case

There can be a bakery in the town

And a dry cleaner and a mayor's office

and a car wash

It's up to you

It's your town

You could be a mother You could

be a son You could be

principal of a junior high school

You get the gist   Pistol cocked

a vigilante hunches

in a crowd The medic sutures

whichever wound next needs tending

Remember there is light

and there is darkness Every night

the townspeople

are cut down in their houses

or in the street But who

has time to mourn the dead

during business hours

even if you are a mother

Life goes on There are decisions to make

the suspicious to be put away

No one wants the job

but there has to be a cop

in the town There

is *good* town

and there is *bad* town

and the rules say only

the cop can tell which from which

which is never not the case

The Country

How silent this neighborhood is.
How vacant and silent.
And thank God it is, that it isn't

LA or New York, where there is very little
—scratch that, *nothing*—
that you miss. What could you miss?

Certainly not the noise
of semi after semi
dragging their big tankers

along the slow lane of the 10 freeway, the BQE.
Not the erratic sprinklers
which, by now, have stopped hissing.

Not the ugly, brown grass.
It's Tuesday.
You'd take Watseka to walk to work.

The cross outside St. Mary's would still be lit,
the organist warming the organ,
tapping the pedals, gently, with his foot.

Most cars on the Tuesday side
of the street would be gone—to clear a path
for the street sweeper. To avoid a pink slip

pinned beneath your windshield wiper,
fluttering, the way sadness flutters,
to get your attention.

No one would miss that.
On Cardiff, you'd pass the miserable bedroom set
someone set out on the lawn,

or you were the bedroom set:
mattress, dresser and nightstand
(both missing drawers), body-length mirror

(half the glass smashed out)—
wasn't that funny, though, how
unfinished you appeared? But not

here; here there are no toilets
stacked in front of an apartment building,
no pot-holed roads.

There's no Farmer's Market on Third
serving stuffed crêpes
you've never tasted.

It isn't raining.
Remember how it was always raining
the night before you left?

And thank God you left.
Aren't there better things
one can do than sleep?

See, how
you now have everything
you need?

Sisyphus: To-do List

Monday crossed off. It's been
crossed off, it seems, forever.
Tuesday—move the Buick. Again,

to the opposite side of the street. At sun-
rise if possible, or if you know better.
Monday crossed off. It's been

that way since way back when
it seems, though he can't remember.
Tuesday—move the Buick. Again?

Outside the sun has barely risen.
Someone has, on his desk calendar,
crossed Monday off. But it wasn't

him. At least he doesn't think it
was, though what has his thinking mattered—
if it's Tuesday, you move the Buick again.

Outside—the sun, the barely risen
form of it, and another
Monday crossed off. As if its task were finished.
His Tuesday moves like a dead Buick again.

Self Portrait as the Movie *Inception*

It's pouring. You can't hail a cab. No, you're on a train. Quite dry, the red wine swishes in a plastic cup. Maybe you're asleep. No, when do you sleep? Wake up, there's a butcher knife on the wood cutting block, so clean and sharp. Is this a dream? Your wife's laid her head on the tracks again—they thrum. *Come lie with me,* she says. No. You have no wife. Somehow she's jimmied the safe in the hotel room. Something small and costly you keep leaving there. Wake. Up. Stupid. Look around you, these ruins *you* built. No, you're the ruin, the city in shambles. Here's your quiet house, grass still green and wet. Your daughter playing in a square of sunlight. No, her little voice spirals through the phone receiver. *When are you coming home?* No. Your daughter's grown now. You call her name, she bolts away. You call, she bolts, her face distorted (A dream?). You wait for the kick. Elevator rigged to explode, you wait. You can't get home, no, not without the music.

Where the View Was Clearer

Had I not chosen to live there—
among the oaks and birches,

trees I'd only ever seen in poems
until then...spruce, pine,

among the jack-in-the-pulpit
(though I much preferred "lady slipper"),

the tiger lily, milkweed, the chickadee
and blue jay, even the pesky squirrel

that toppled the feeder in the backyard?
There were organic farm stands

with FRESH CORN,
and I had a job lined up

with excellent dental,
so I should have felt satisfied,

in that way I was taught
God was satisfied

after (like any father, I would guess)
He'd finished with all His work

because He saw everything
was good—the world

we were in, and part of,
so we could marvel and point

to our heart's content
if we wanted—to the conifer,

the pond with its still water,
the frog leaping, its splash

right out of a book
of haiku. My wife asked,

What are you thinking?
or *What's the matter?* but

I was a stand of trees by then. Impenetrable
as the wood from which I imagined

Bishop's moose first emerged,
otherworldly, taking shape

in my mind even now, though
I've never actually *seen* a moose,

only signs warning of moose,
and NO PASSING ZONE signs

as we drove Route 9 to the trail.
If it was indulgent to take it all in—

what *that* flower was called,
which was edible or toxic,

which should never be touched,
such useful information—

the way one might take in breath,
slowly, almost without effort,

then I was indulgent. And why not be?
Nothing seemed to threaten to kill me

here. No careless hunter. No bear.
Just us, the trees, and contentment,

unfamiliar as it all felt, having come
of age in a part of the country where

the sun didn't so much glint
as glared, and there seemed

no shelter from it. This was
the '80s, in Joshua Tree.

Tom & Jerry on the TV. Mountains
everywhere else. From that

house, I could still point out the rock-
face I slid down once, because

my stepfather shouted,
shouted my name from its base—

I was dead. He was
going to kill me. I

had lost track of
time and lost

my brother, or
left him behind on

a boulder
to watch our

gallon jug
of water, our bag

of green apples,
because he wouldn't

climb any
farther, even so

close to the peak, maybe
didn't want to

see what was just
below, in the valley,

or beyond
the ridge, where

the view was
clearer and farther, but

I had to
see if it matched

what I imagined
and had

no time
to spare, not

with my stepfather's
voice below—he was

was going to kill me
if the rattlesnake hadn't.

Or my scraped elbow.
My shredded knee.

And we walked back in silence,
he and I, like Abraham

and Isaac must have
after leaving what had to be left

on the mountain, after Isaac saw
what his father was

capable of, the price
of obedience, which I paid

that day while my brother watched
E.T. and would not look at me. *Ouch,*

the alien said, its finger pulsing
like the lightning bugs

here on the trail as evening begins.
How even to describe it,

which seems my duty alone?
My wife and I walked, and I was silent

as a distant mountain
where something important

might have been lost.
Do you like it out here?

she asked—the steep ascent, bony trees
we used like trekking poles, the skittish

deer or chipmunk bounding off,
the poisoned oak. She hoped I liked it,

wherever I was in thought.
And I think I did, I wanted to.

Though I might have left that boy
on the mountain, caught in a thicket,

long ago. You should have seen it
up there, I told her. From the peak,

looking down into the grassy valley,
unexpected after so much

sand and cactus needle. I watched,
for what seemed an eternity—

it was like some new holy land,
some long promise—clouds parting,

low rumble of thunder, then
light, a voice, however garbled—

finally fulfilled. I wish
you could've seen it, I said.

You'd have hardly believed—
a family of rams, I swear,

in the valley, in the desert,
unbothered and unchanging, and still

there I bet. Grazing. Eating their fill.

Myth of the Bear

That winter, snow dusted the hemlock, each spiked cone.
Snow salted my hair—it was that long, that winter.
A black bear cub curled beside me, hers a dark, honeyed sleep.
If this were a fable, one could sleep the whole winter

without interruption, that's how long it felt as the bear cub
and I kept each other warm. She had no clamp, no shackle
or trap marks in her fur, of course I checked. Carefully,
I peeled fat, gray ticks from her back, but I was gentle

then. Sometimes it was my turn to wade
waist-deep into the river, and that was fine. If we were
lucky, there were fish, though no fish would
consider this luck. Sometimes the bear cub seemed to stalk

a smell, sniffing, I assumed her mother, but it could
have been anything, that winter. You wonder what
there is to learn here, other than this is not a fable.
Other than, whenever I woke, the bear was always a bear again.

Now that I live in this part of the country,

the fireflies are far
more abundant—a word

I thought I'd never use
again, and someone says,

how beautiful, which I
could forgive, and someone

says, *look, they*
flash the way hazard

lights sometimes flash...
and I might have said, no,

don't they seem to pulse
with the glow of old

grievances? But then,
no one really asked me.

The World Is Full

I saw the wolf outside the window. In
the backyard, near the park bench nearly

stripped of all its paint. Or I thought
it was a wolf I saw, insomuch as I even called

wolfwolf through every room of the farmhouse—
it was quite the spectacle. *False alarm,*

one might say, as if explanation were a kind
of comfort. I was not comforted.

My panic startled me, the way one can
be startled by something he's read in a book

he's forgotten he owns, that he can't,
in the slightest, remember buying

while thumbing over the other spines,
all those titles huddled together there

on the shelves—out of nowhere, we say,
in these cases, *where did this come from, how*

had I missed this...the wolf seemed to come
out of nowhere, or maybe from a book

I remember read to me as a child.
Some cautionary tale. A window capable of being

looked in, seen through, if you were brave.
It was not a wolf outside the window, it was

a coyote. But with a wolf's bulk. Its metallic flash
of fur, its appetite. I admit, I was afraid.

Not for myself. But for the chickens.
I looked out the window because the chickens

clucked so madly, like children at a school
running amok—the hens flapped at the glass.

The chicks, instinctively, slipped out
of sight into the taller wet grass. No, it was

not a wolf. Of course, I knew the difference.
I had been a boy. Been small enough

to be clenched in a wolf's jaw, though
I never was. I was safe. I wanted to save them

but the commercial in the background insisted
the window for savings was closing fast,

then faded to black as they do when they're
done. The wolf scattered them. The way

feathers can be scattered, torn from the body.
Or the way children are drilled, even in grade

school, to scatter, *shhhh, we've prepared
for this now*—I called *wolf*, I clapped

at the glass which, I've been told, makes
a difference, and I wanted

things to be different. To the chickens,
it must have looked as if I took delight

in their predicament, and who would tell
them otherwise? The world is full of suffering,

it's true; why not delight in that
it's yours, not mine, for once? The coyote

slunk away, or the wolf did, something
dead, I thought, between its teeth. I was

afraid, though I went out to look for what
was missing, what was lost to the woods.

Ten chickens, two chicks. I counted
them, like I tally all loss, scattered

the way one might scatter birdseed
in the yard, or how one might scatter

a child's ashes to the ocean's indifference.
I had been a boy. Lost among the woods

as in some fable. Or maybe not lost. Just the shade
of tree bark. Not a wolf, though to the chickens

the distinction hardly matters.
*Here, chickee, chickee...*No one

had bothered to name them. To name
them, we believed, would make them

harder to kill and eat, but how
wrong we were. I believed

I could save them, or that saving them
meant I loved them, that my love was good

for something.

The Adventures of Huckleberry Finn

was first banned in Concord, Massachusetts, in 1885.
If you haven't read it,
it's the story of two runaways—
one from an abusive drunk, the other
slavery. Not a terribly strange story—
a boy leaves home, flees
the few bedsheets snapping on the clothesline,
that appear to be ghosts. But these days,
everyone is haunted by something. A smile.
The thing someone said. I live in Amherst, Massachusetts,
haunted by the name of Lord Jeffery Amherst who,
it has been said, distributed smallpox-infected blankets
and handkerchiefs to Native Americans
(he might have said "savages") surrounding his fort.
How many stories open that way?
With some simple exchange.
With some naming. *Bee. Bullfrog. Catalpa.*
Lily pad. Nigger—even now,
see how a name can stick? Or swat
like a stick? I was never assigned *Huck Finn*
when I was a kid, and my kid has never read it,
though had she, she may have read the version
that exchanges "nigger" for "slave"—
a softening, so they say, like inventing a farm upstate

for the dog that, maybe having tracked
some far-off sound or movement,
has been crushed by a speeding car, *bad dog...*
A dog needs a lot of space to run with other dogs,
and without a leash, you explain.
Even a child, you think, should understand that.

The flowers

in the greenhouse
now flowers

in the supermarket
rubber-bound

clipped
from wherever

they seemed almost
to nod

their agreement with what
the breeze once said

now flowers
in some glass vase

on the dining room table
where no one eats

What race they are
doesn't matter nor if

their stems are thorny
you see

They're just flowers
They die

You walk by
them all the time

hardly thinking
twice about their names

Labor Day: Brighton Beach

How lovely, at last, to have nothing to do but sit, shirtless, in my
collapsible chair, reading Gerald Stern's *American Sonnets*, and lovely to sit,
beer in my lap, just a little tipsy, lovely, too, to ignore beauty, or desire, or
whatever, the young woman unfolding her nylon tent, smacking each stake
into the sand with her sandal's heel, slipping discretely into her swimsuit,
though I could watch the plane zip past, tugging a banner for *Wicked*,
which there was still time to see if you wanted, or the sailboat glide slowly
by, and it was a good day for sailing, a good day, so I didn't have to think
about sorrow or loss, though, let's face it, I did, how not to—the old man
missing a left leg—not how it happened, or when—but if it gets easier, you
know, living with it, crutch snug under each armpit, and Jill had been gone
a long time to warm her goat curry, then farther out, a jet ski, like a straight
razor, slits the water's surface, Carmen already asleep under a sun hat.

Midlife Aubade

There's a certain comfort
in knowing a bridge has stood

almost forever. There
long before the dawn's first

foghorn blast—like one beast
lowing to another—

and before each ship I could describe now
with painstaking precision

that will glide slowly
underneath. Steel. Suspension wire.

Something in my life
should compare to these ... Once

there was a bridge whose name
I never learned, under which

a small stream shimmered
the way a pond sometimes shimmers

for a moment, when a child flips a coin into it.
Tiny fish swam there. But the water

was like smoke. I thought,
nothing should have to live like this.

Nocturne from the North Carolina Aquarium
at Pine Knoll Shores

Mop head wrung.
Vacuum tube coiled.
Snow-capped tortoise shells
slipped, like glaciers,
slowly out of sight.

Quiet now
inside the bell
of the moon
jellyfish, the lonely cone
of the hermit crab.

Inside the night hours
left to be swept,
which is the man's job.
It is his job to buff
away the child's cheek

or palm print
that's smudged the glass
of the exhibit tank
for the largemouth bass,
which reads "it is known

to take any bait it considers alive."
Some have been found,
it read, their mouths punctured,
from being caught and let go,
let go so many times.

ii.

Days after the Election, We Finally Discuss the Weather

some of us discuss it

    some are silent

        outside had grown gravely cold

Freddie retouches with white paint

    scuff marks on the bar cabinet the garden wall

        how he pines for the African sun

it never feels like my home here he says

    I want to believe he means climate but I know

        it never feels like my home here he says

how he pines for the African sun

    scuff marks on the bar cabinet the garden wall

        Freddie retouches with white paint

outside had grown gravely cold

some are silent

some of us discuss it

They said I was an alternate,

so I thought like an alternate
Answered *black* when asked

where is the nearest bathroom,
guilty

as charged when
the barista called the name

I made up, only
half-expecting judgment

My new way
I mostly liked

until the bailiff said, *silence*
your cellphones

or *you have*
the right to remain silent,

to which I felt compelled
to raise my right hand

They said I was an alternate,

which meant I could be
anyone, everyone, really

For example, in one version,
I was the custodian
for the 19th floor

Had to set out
a CAUTION sign

(you know—
stick figure, black,
tumbling down into a hole)

so when I
got to the courthouse

early, I'd
see it, and say,
careful now, watch

your step
to myself,
but who

the hell did I think I was

They said I was an alternate,

so I sought to perfect
silence as was

expected of me
I nodded

in the lobby,
said nothing

with my breakfast
interrogated

on the conveyor belt
Then the elevator sealed

me like an envelope
At dinner, my partner

poured the bottle
of wine I pointed to,

which also helped
Pulling open

the can of wet food
was conversation

enough for the cat
If I could tell her,

my mother might
be most impressed—

So, all that practice
finally paid off, huh

How like a god,
they will say

of it—useless,
and everlasting

The sentence

begins with its subject,
   which is the sentence.

Track the sentence
   to find out what happens

or how it will act. It is
   the subject, after all. To track,

meaning *keep an eye on*,
   which is synecdoche,

part representing the whole
   of a thing. One

may track a package if he pleases.
   One may track a person,

though you'd probably want
   the whole of him, not only

an eye, or perhaps
   only an eye. Look how

the sentence is so capable
of embracing contraction.

A him may function
as a subject, but that depends

upon the sentence, i.e., A man
is subject to his sentence.

You understand.
Such syntax renders it like

a package showing evidence
of having been tampered with—

They said I was an alternate,

said the case was in the bag,

                open and shut, they said

he was black, there was a gun,

                or gun plus black equals him

A no-brainer,

                they said No question

he was black They said,

                do the math, dummy,

doesn't it add up If you think,

                they said Think

of our children Our children

                They said, oh, never mind

They said I was an alternate

They called an officer as a witness
They called an officer as a witness
They called an officer as a witness
They called another officer as a witness

and another, yes, an officer
Knock, knock Who's there *An officer,*
of course (Can *I* get a witness)
They called one—an officer It was

like watching the saddest floats of a parade pass
They called an officer as a witness
and again, instructed us *You sit*
there now, like good little children,

and listen Listen good, children, they said,
as if we might soon be tested

They said I was an alternate

but before that *what do you like to do*

with your free time and one of us said long walks

with her dog around the park and another

said kick it with the homies on the block

and I might have said cook or write or something

dumb like that though the judge didn't judge

and another juror would only answer

in private and one said he liked to read

a good book (though what one considers good

is arguable) and sure the question

seemed odd but it took our minds off

the past awhile which we all had

to answer for (or to) one said take a warm

bath one whispered are we ever going home

They said I was an alternate

unless I, my cat, anyone
I'd sat next to
on the bus
or a park bench, I,
or anyone
who took the first
sip of my drink,
had ever been accused
of a crime,
or convicted
of a crime, if I
ever touched
a yellow strip of tape,
ever watched *Cops*,
oddly, a theme song
I could recite
before I could
even say *run*,
according to my mother,
who was, since I am
still under oath,
sure, the victim
of a crime,
then another crime

You've heard this before
I've told it
fair, impartial
as a pixelated face

They said I was an alternate

and brought me to the other room

with the other alternates

where we couldn't hear

what might have been whispered

about evidence

or guilt by the others,

though I did

press my ear to the quiet

wall as if listening

for the tumblers of a bank vault

They said I was an alternate

and looked closely
at the defendant,

the way a jeweler might
inspect what he's been

sold to be a diamond,
then looked at me

again They said,
Do you understand

They said I was an alternate,

said, *thank you*

for your service,

though what

had I done

They said I was an alternate,

said here, a dozen eggs
Twelve strips of bacon

Twelve pads of butter, softening
Twelve mouths to feed

One smoking pan, one me
Twelve bowls or plates,

whichever they prefer
The forks and knives

all accusingly aimed
at the ceiling fan

which turns
as slow as a mind might turn

Twelve pairs of eyes
dark and unblinking

Twelve mouths to feed
One me

They said I was an alternate,

but that's all
behind me now

Today, I'm around the table
with friends, finally

Dungeons and Dragons
night, building

a character
for a campaign

that will likely kill me
I hardly talk

about the old days anymore
The DM asks my name,

my backstory, my flaw,
which I have left to either

fate or chance
What's the difference

In the end,
what damage there is is

largely psychic, is all
in the mind, which is

not to say imaginary
even in roleplay,

and I, for one, play
by the book

I roll the dice
I take what I get

They said I was an alternate

ending for the end
        already predestined

No one would argue
        with the fact of

his blackness
        Not even

me my pen sharpened
        the way

some pitchforks are sharpened
        in the parable

I don't remember
        the lesson of

if there was a lesson
        if it wasn't just another story

without consequence
        Nothing

to walk away
　　　with Inherit

or pass down

iii.

Sergeant Al Powell, 30 Years Later

Fictional, sure,
but his story

is no different
from the others

A toy gun...
I didn't know...

And the boy
had no name

you could sew
into a tee shirt,

minor character
that he was,

Powell too,
who, I

should probably add,
was black

as a steel-toed boot,
obedient as a Saint

Bernard or night-
stick, though what

else did I expect,
what had I paid

to see in this dark
that I hadn't already seen

At the Park, a Boy's Birthday Party

No surprises here, really.
Not the plastic,

white cutlery
or the fancy glass bowl,

cubes of pineapple
and Bosc pear

floating in punch
(naturally red)

that no one
(thank the Lord)

has thought yet to spike.
Each boy, blindfolded,

spun in place, and shoved
down the piñata's path

with a bat
he can barely lift,

the piñata star-shaped,
tasseled pink at its ends,

seems accurate.
At this age,

their limbs
inarticulate as the smoke

of catfish or pork ribs
that hiss on the park grill.

They hardly notice
the sun's descent.

It's getting late, I think
to say as someone's father

knots the blindfold
over my eyes. Fits the bat

into my hands. In my ear,
the boys shriek, and there—

the star,
snagged in the oak

of my mind, the rope,
swaying

almost gently. How,
even dizzied,

do I step towards it?

What You Call It

Not my usual route to the market—past
the railroad tracks, then past

Grace Episcopal Church,
its courtyard empty—no men

clasping hands as though agreeing,
finally, to the difficult terms

of some treaty—so I would not
have known it was a peach tree

unless the person who planted it
or someone on the street

told me. Which is not to say
its fruit didn't look

peach-like—it did...
rather I didn't read it as such, didn't

know what I was
seeing, really—from where I stood

the fruit perfect and young
and heavy, at least heavy enough

to bow the branches, though hardly
ready yet to eat. *Ripe,*

one might say, which, true,
is more precise—precision

a thing of value. Not that
the fruit cares what you call it.

Or stands for anything
other than what time can make

of some small human intervention.
Is no piece of literature.

The peach was simply a peach,
and there for the taking,

which is often said of an object that has gone
unwatched for too long, susceptible

to trespass, which happens
first in the mind, and happened first

because of fruit,
or so says The Good Book

if you believe in such things. Knowledge,
which a poet once called "historical," too

a trespassing of sorts, the proof of which
perhaps best shown in how one

might punish a slave who had been
taught to read the word *beauty* or *toil*

or *rest*, secretly, and by firelight.
There are things nearly impossible

to forget, having so trespassed,
having badly needed to see up close

this tree fixed in place, its fruit
dangling—there

within reach, though not
the same as being offered.

Tenderness, I have learned,
is only one test

of whether some fruit
has fully ripened. *You*

press the flesh right here. But for me,
that would mean crossing

half the yard the way a paper boat
might be pushed, by wind, across a pond.

Myth of the Lighthouse

The story begins with a beacon
in a tower of brick.
Or it begins with a man,

you'd call him *the keeper*,
who mostly refuses
sleep to listen

to the steady crash
of the Pacific or the red buoy's
sad clanging inside the mist.

It begins with brick,
wheelbarrows of bricks
someone must stack

into the shape of a story.
The night was too black
for stars. The light

failed; the man slept. The rest
you should already know.
How silly we were

to trust in man, but then
who hasn't made that mistake?
Inside the mist, the red buoy

clangs its sadness,
the man asleep;
that's how the story begins.

The Ferry

I still had a lover. Maybe let's start there.
I hitched a ride to Boston, where I missed

the ferry by what seemed like minutes. But time
can work that way in the mind. I was in love

or wanted to be in love and there was distance
everywhere is maybe a better way to put it,

though what exactly was *it*, I hadn't given it
a designation. I looked for the boat, it wasn't there:

only the dock, a few seagulls, a blue distance.
If I was supposed to wave goodbye, I missed

my chance, though what did I care, so in love
with solitude, at least I was at the time.

It seemed easy, being lonely, watching time
lapse, that boat long dispatched, I'd missed it

yet there I was waving, like a fool in love
perhaps, at what? I couldn't tell. I wasn't there

when the ferry left, remember, I missed
it, or they went on without me. The distance

made it hard to see clearly where distance
ended, or if it did. Or I didn't make it in time

to see, maybe time was against me. I missed
the ferry, I had no money. The ferryman said *It*

was fine and smiled at me. Smiled. There
was the shore and me wanting to be in love

though I wasn't. I carried what I could. Love?
I didn't have room for it. In the distance,

I swore my solitude waved. I missed it where
I was headed, sure, but there was hardly time

for that. The boat was early. I boarded it
and stood on the stern. Part of me was missing,

but there had to be a cost. That part I missed—
my mind a rough sea I might have loved

watching lap were I not so inside it—
my mind the fish, too, the shore distant

as the voice I thought I heard in it, as time
itself. The ferry was late. I was there

hoping I missed it. I didn't trust the distance,
lovely as it seemed. I didn't trust time

nor where it carried me. I knew what was there.

Aubade Ending with a Pacemaker

It's so easy, from the hotel's twelfth floor,
to see the sheet of ice splinter, then drift

like continents on the river. From this height,
the snow flurries, doesn't seem to fall at all. Maybe

it's the trucks delivering meat (packed
in salt, I imagine), gliding slowly along

that make me think back on the La Brea
Bakery truck driver whose heart quit

at the intersection of Melrose and Western.
Paramedics listened to his chest. Blew

and blew into his mouth before he was wound
to a stretcher, rushed away—the truck, all

its freshly baked baguettes, left and, I was almost
certain, stolen. Who knows

if anything can really be saved? Not you
or me. Not the heart—unreliable

little engine it is. It shouldn't be a surprise
when I say, "the La Brea Bakery truck driver,"

that I'm thinking of you.

Myth of the Cow

If you see one, lazing in an open field
of grass, alone,

                expect rain
I've been told—though I may have added

the loneliness part myself
(you know how I

can't resist loneliness)—still
who would've believed it, even

when we saw her—the cow—such calm
and silence, sprawled, almost expectant,
in the yellowing field,

                even after it rained
just as you, so many times, said it would?

Multiple Choice

Dull, bulky, previously owned, it was
usually tucked in my backpack
next to *Algebra* or *Earth Science*, and my gym shorts—
US History. Some old scene drawn

on the cover. There was a teacher,
a classroom number, I was this
many years old. There was time, which was
set aside every day. I had a locker,

a combination. I sat at a distance
that softened the edges of white chalk
on the board (poor vision) though even
that didn't make me much care to commit

the past to memory except to darken
the right bubble on the test sheet—
Christopher Columbus discovered
America in _____;

The Declaration of Independence
was first signed by _____;
_____ assassinated Abraham Lincoln.
Answers were simple and dependable.

Black and white. You were remembered,
for better or worse, for what you did, what
you refused to do—every year, Rosa Parks
sat unmoved, Dr. King dreamed, and I

recorded it, as if for the first time. I've heard
textbook sometimes used to describe an act
as flat and predictable as a stretch
of country road—miles of the same

cow lying in cut grass, slowly chewing cud
with the effort or patience it might take
to grind the difficulty of any fact down.
Robert E. Lee surrendered at _____

to end the Civil War. At the end,
my mother once said, every battle
is lost by someone, has its casualties.
Bronze monuments erected

to the story, or some other
old scene just as dull and clunky.
Until _____, years before
I met my wife, I could have been

dragged off for simply glancing at her—
which I do often and too long. The moral?
Who knows? Maybe, if you're lucky,
you outlive the usefulness of such knowledge.

Besides, it's a new world. I own
The Riverside Shakespeare. Two biographies
of Coleridge. My shelves lined with the past
and its usual despairs. Its joys as well.

Sometimes I look. Sometimes
I get swept up in all the looking. There
is rain. Someone returns home.
A letter arrives with the expected news.

A cat, on the window sill, asleep.
My wife in a rocking chair. Quietly
reading. Everyone keeps asking when
we will finally have a baby,

because it's a thing we can choose
now. I mean, how lucky is that?

Love Poem

The tennis match was still on
and while some watched, some sat around
and shucked oysters, cut them from their shells,
the score going in the background—Love, 15, 30, etc...
A peculiar system, though what
did I know, certainly not the name
of either player, how many games were left,

or what each white boundary line meant.
Only that love meant nothing in tennis,
or didn't exactly mean "nothing"
but rather "to have nothing." Zero. One
hardly thinks of love as bad except when tennis is on,
when one considers a score is being kept.
I've certainly seen this
                              to be true more than once.
I'll say, love is no good, but context is important.
Okay—my love and I sipped bourbon late
one night. She had been pregnant
with twins, belly a greater zero. Some said, *Love
made them*, and that was true. And after, some said,
Well, at least you still have love, and that was also true.

Moths

It's hard not to think of them
    as stupid. I know. I too

        have watched these spare few
    bump the lamp fixture

outside *Floyd's*, under which
    a man lights a woman's cigarette

        with his own, or a moth
    floats too close to the soft blue

hum of a bug zapper. How could they
    know better—the moon, tonight, so full

        of confusion. Believe me,
    I know. *It seems*

you've lost your way home, the text may have said.
    Again. Or *it seems you're lost again,*

        the text said, *home*
    this way. Perhaps. Enough bourbon

or sadness will do that.
        Enough moonlight.

                It's a misfiring of synapses taking place,
        of course—the moth triangulates its navigation

through the moon, then drunkenly
        flutters into the little flame you've kindled

                with split wood and an old blues tune;
        couldn't have known better,

and better off, all of them, before
        I arrived, with something

                like desire, this edge
of flint anxious to be struck.

Against Melancholy

At first it *is*
Beethoven's Ninth

I'm thinking of—
not all of it—mostly

the fourth movement,
that rousing crescendo

you might hear
at the end of a movie

where the protagonist
has graduated or overcome

some great hurdle,
cello, violin, then flute,

brass, layering
one another, swelling

towards that feeling
of triumph

I so rarely seem to have,
but often think about,

now maybe
because of the shrieks

and cheers from a party
in the courtyard,

drifting into the window
of my room, where

I'm often alone,
laughter rising

like fireworks, then
I'm thinking of

the feeling itself,
joy, how

it almost seems made
of air, like you

can be full of it,
or sometimes

it's a child's
red bouncing ball

that somehow gets away
from you, and you

have to chase it
into a busy intersection,

and everyone's
laying on their horns,

all that air
vibrating and swollen,

your chest swollen, too,
and maybe chasing it

could get you killed
or crippled at best,

but what feels better
than that moment,

when you catch it,
when it's yours?

A Public Service Announcement

In 2019, Kentucky enacted an abortion ban,

and Missouri enacted an abortion ban,

and Alabama did it too, and Georgia

also enacted an abortion ban—because

shouldn't every child be offered

at least a shot, however small, at this life?

In the Gardening Section of Home Depot

The question is, of course, how could one not
think of *Romeo and Juliet* (as clichéd as that
may sound)—with you, high atop an orange ladder,

and all the potted ferns in bloom, or whatever they were,
though what could it matter, seeing that they were
all fake. I'm sorry, I didn't get your name. Your assistance
was beautiful, and yes, I found the caulk

needed to patch the ruined wall, the wall I ruined
trying to hang my Audrey Hepburn still.
Who calls photos "stills" anymore? People must

think that antiquated, like saying *eros* when
you mean *desire*. I'm sorry, I didn't get your name,
though I suppose it's good to have a place
to pat and smooth with a spade, a place to leave,

a place to return to. And no, I wasn't certain
of your return policy, but who's really sure
about anything? What could go wrong? And besides,

I try not to return purchases, even if I'm unhappy
with them. I'm sorry I didn't get your name

but believe it was as beautiful as the swatch of
robin's egg or swatch of apricot I pocketed,

because it's good to leave with something, isn't it?
Time-card punched and apron slipped, like
snake-husk, over a hook. I should talk you down

from that ladder. Say here, take my hand. I know
all too well how the store must feel, emptied.
After everyone has left, and its letters still burn.
Take my hand. What could possibly go wrong?

Love Elegy with Sunoco and *Rand McNally Road Atlas*

Over there,
       there are fields
              of yellowed
      grass, and trees,
all nondescript,
      and a snow
             mound shrinking,
      though there
is no boy tussling
      in the snow,
             no leaves
      stuck to his
thick wool cap
      and mittens, no,
             not in this
      weather, no
mother looking
      sternly on, no,
             nothing like
      that exactly,
just the field,
      the inevitable
             turning of leaves—
      a sound

I can almost
        feel even with
                the window
        raised, or so
I'd like to
        believe, though
                I can't quite
        feel it, not
the way I feel
        your hand
                touching
        the bag
of dried mango
        at the same
                time as mine,
        oh, the luck
of that, and
        luck too that
                no one has
        struck a deer
for many miles
        now, the bare
                road, what isn't
        slumped there,

the same

    kind of proof

        as the needle,

    bright and

trembling, just

    above the E

        on the fuel

    gauge, which points

to a specific

    emptiness, one

        surely necessary

    to address,

though I can see,

    with increasing

        clarity, all

    that's left

the frame,

    everything already

        in the past

    tense, even us,

and simpler that

    way, to somehow

        ignore the cold,

    and the cost

slowly climbing
     at the pump
          right before
     the nozzle's click,
or the soft light
     of the phone,
          and your face—
     so briefly lit
and filling up
     the window.

Poem from a Rest Stop Diner

There is one story and one story only
—Robert Graves

which ends up being
the same diner and the same
men licking the same

finger before turning
the page of yesterday's
paper, always reading

yesterday's paper because
it costs so little to look
back, to have your mug

refilled with black coffee
cooled under a ceiling fan's
spin. Nothing is unexpected,

and it's absolutely perfect,
down to the waitress
wearing her name

permanently marked on
a plastic heart she's pinned
over her heart, her finger

slipped in the ceramic ring
of the mug. The bill,
like a whisper, tucked beneath

your plate. The bell at the
host stand, the little girl
smacking it, though not

to get anyone's attention—
just to hear it sing, the same
song, the only song

it knows.

Notes

Dr. John Henrik Clarke, to whom this book's initial epigraph is attributed, was a Pan-Africanist writer, historian, professor, and a pioneer in the creation of Africana studies and professional institutions in academia starting in the late 1960s.

This book's final epigraph was excerpted from poet Jennifer Chang's brilliant and illuminating 2019 lecture, "Other Pastorals: Writing Race and Place," delivered at the Bread Loaf Environmental Writers' Conference on June 1, 2019.

"*Boy Pulling a Thorn from His Foot*": The sculpture observed in the poem was entitled *Spinario (Boy Pulling a Thorn from His Foot)*, by Antico (Italian, Mantua ca. 1460–1528), and was on display at The Metropolitan Museum of Art, New York.

"Mafia Myth": Mafia is a popular game, also known as Werewolves, Night in Palermo, or Assassins. The game was developed by Dmitry Davidoff in 1987 at the Psychology Department of Moscow State University, who was a psychology teacher at the time.

"The World is Full" owes a debt to poet Sarah Anderson and The Word Barn, located in Exeter, NH.

"[They said I was an alternate]": At the end of July 2018, I served two weeks on jury duty in Kings County, New York. The charge was attempted murder, the defendant a young, black male. However, I was selected for jury duty as an "alternate," meaning I would attend every session of the trial but when it came time to deliberate, I, and the other alternates, would have no input on the potential verdict, and would be placed in a separate room altogether during the deliberation. The 13-poem "alternate" sequence emerged from that experience.

"Sergeant Al Powell, 30 Years Later": Sergeant Al Powell is an LAPD cop who helps John McClane with the terrorist takeover of the Nakatomi Plaza in the 1988 film *Die Hard*, which celebrated its 30-year anniversary in 2018. The poem is in memoriam of Tamir Rice.

"Against Melancholy": The finale of Beethoven's Symphony No. 9—"Ode to Joy"—was adapted from Friedrich Schiller's poem of the same title.

Acknowledgments

My unending gratitude to the editors and editorial teams of the following journals in which the poems in this book, sometimes in earlier versions, first appeared: *The Baffler*; *The Common*; *Connotation Press: An Online Artifact*; *Foundry*; *Green Mountains Review*; *Iron Horse Literary Review*; *Matter*; *METRO arte+literature*; *On the Seawall*; *Poem-a-Day*; *Poetry Northwest*; *The Rumpus*; *The Southeast Review*; *Tinderbox Poetry Journal*; *upstreet*; *Waxwing*; *West Branch Wired*; *Yes, Poetry*; and *Zocalo Public Square*.

I have had the great fortune of an amazing community of friends, artists, and thinkers who have encouraged and supported the work collected in this book. Major thanks to Caroline Mar, Jennifer Funk, Michael Jarmer, Matt Donovan, Oliver de la Paz, Carl Phillips, my dear brother, Tommye Blount, John Murillo, Diane Seuss, Francine Conley, Michael Mercurio, Sarah Audsley, Virginia Konchan, Heather Tresseler, Carly Joy Miller, Jennifer Franklin, John Hennessy, Phillip B. Williams, Kerrin McCadden, Dawn Potter, Keith Leonard, Jennifer Sperry Steinorth, Patrick Donnelly, Matthew Olzmann, Vievee Francis, Patricia Smith, my wonderful peers and friends at the M.F.A. Program for Writers at Warren Wilson, and my incredible Cave Canem family. And that isn't everyone. . . I know I've overlooked some important folks here. Please forgive me and know that I appreciate you.

Major thanks to Rashaun Rucker for allowing us to use "Finally Free" as the collection's cover art. His entire American Ornithology series is captivating and poignant. I'm so very grateful.

To Jessica Jo Starr, it seems only by luck, magic, or grace, perhaps all three, that I have you as a partner in this life, to be showered by the constancy of your love, affection, brilliance, and generosity. This book is for you, and for our girls, Bridghette and Zora Jo.

Lastly, though certainly far from least, a huge thank you to Martha Rhodes, Ryan Murphy, Bridget Bell, Hannah Matheson, and the entire Four Way family, for their continued support of my work. This collection is incredibly important to me. Thank you for believing in it and me.

Nathan McClain was born and raised in the lower desert of Southern California. He is the author of *Scale* (Four Way Books, 2017), a recipient of fellowships from The Frost Place, Sewanee Writers' Conference, Bread Loaf Writers' Conference, and a graduate of the M.F.A. Program for Writers at Warren Wilson. A Cave Canem fellow, his poems and prose have recently appeared or are forthcoming in *Poetry Northwest*, *Green Mountains Review*, *Guesthouse*, *The Common*, and *The Critical Flame*, among others. He is an Assistant Professor of Creative Writing and African American Literary Arts at Hampshire College and serves as poetry editor of the *Massachusetts Review*.

Publication of this book was made possible by grants and donations. We are also grateful to those individuals who participated in our 2021 Build a Book Program. They are:

Anonymous (16), Maggie Anderson, Susan Kay Anderson, Kristina Andersson, Kate Angus, Kathy Aponick, Sarah Audsley, Jean Ball, Sally Ball, Clayre Benzadón, Greg Blaine, Laurel Blossom, adam bohannon, Betsy Bonner, Lee Briccetti, Joan Bright, Jane Martha Brox, Susan Buttenwieser, Anthony Cappo, Carla and Steven Carlson, Paul and Brandy Carlson, Renee Carlson, Alice Christian, Karen Rhodes Clarke, Mari Coates, Jane Cooper, Ellen Cosgrove, Peter Coyote, Robin Davidson, Kwame Dawes, Michael Anna de Armas, Brian Komei Dempster, Renko and Stuart Dempster, Matthew DeNichilo, Rosalynde Vas Dias, Kent Dixon, Patrick Donnelly, Lynn Emanuel, Blas Falconer, Elliot Figman, Jennifer Franklin, Helen Fremont and Donna Thagard, Gabriel Fried, John Gallaher, Reginald Gibbons, Jason Gifford, Jean and Jay Glassman, Dorothy Tapper Goldman, Sarah Gorham and Jeffrey Skinner, Lauri Grossman, Julia Guez, Sarah Gund, Naomi Guttman and Jonathan Mead, Kimiko Hahn, Mary Stewart Hammond, Beth Harrison, Jeffrey Harrison, Melanie S. Hatter, Tom Healy and Fred Hochberg, K.T. Herr, Karen Hildebrand, Joel Hinman, Deming Holleran, Lillian Howan, Thomas and Autumn Howard, Catherine Hoyser, Elizabeth Jackson, Jessica Jacobs and Nickole Brown, Christopher Johanson, Jen Just, Maeve Kinkead, Alexandra Knox, Lindsay and John Landes, Suzanne Langlois, Laura Lauth, Sydney Lea, David Lee and Jamila Trindle, Rodney Terich Leonard, Jen Levitt, Howard Levy, Owen Lewis, Matthew Lippman, Jennifer Litt, Karen Llagas, Sara London and Dean Albarelli, Clarissa Long, James Longenbach, Cynthia Lowen, Ralph and Mary Ann Lowen, Ricardo Maldonado, Myra Malkin, Jacquelyn Malone, Carrie Mar, Kathleen McCoy, Ellen McCulloch-Lovell, Lupe Mendez, David Miller, Josephine Miller, Nicki Moore, Guna Mundheim, Matthew Murphy and Maura Rockcastle, Michael and Nancy Murphy, Myra Natter, Jay Baron Nicorvo, Ashley Nissler, Kimberly Nunes, Rebecca and Daniel Okrent, Robert Oldshue and Nina Calabresi, Kathleen Ossip, Judith Pacht, Cathy McArthur Palermo, Marcia and Chris Pelletiere, Sam Perkins, Susan Peters and Morgan Driscoll, Patrick Phillips, Robert Pinsky, Megan Pinto, Connie Post, Kyle Potvin, Grace Prasad, Kevin Prufer, Alicia Jo Rabins, Anna Duke Reach,

Victoria Redel, Martha Rhodes, Paula Rhodes, Louise Riemer, Sarah Santner, Amy Schiffman, Peter and Jill Schireson, Roni and Richard Schotter, James and Nancy Shalek, Soraya Shalforoosh, Peggy Shinner, Anita Soos, Donna Spruijt-Metz, Ann F. Stanford, Arlene Stang, Page Hill Starzinger, Marina Stuart, Yerra Sugarman, Marjorie and Lew Tesser, Eleanor Thomas, Tom Thompson and Miranda Field, James Tjoa, Ellen Bryant Voigt, Connie Voisine, Moira Walsh, Ellen Dore Watson, Calvin Wei, John Wender, Eleanor Wilner, Mary Wolf, and Pamela and Kelly Yenser.